# SAQs Into Becoming a USA Federal Contractor in the Top 4 Markets

BY

Marvina Case

# Table of Contents

# A Note from the Author

Ah, the illustrious journey of the multi-hyphenate entrepreneur! Seven companies, you say? Quite the modest collection. I mean, who doesn't have a defense firm, an AI startup, a healthcare venture, and a construction company all under one roof? It's practically the new "I have a dog and a cat" situation. Let's break it down, shall we? Talarai.com is all about defense—because, of course, who wouldn't want to dabble in national security while juggling the complexities of healthcare with MH-360? And then there's Swetspot.AI, where you've presumably figured out how to make technology work smarter, not harder.

And let's not overlook Chocolate Cyclops Construction. I can only imagine the delightful conversations that arise when discussing infostructure (which, let's be honest, sounds like a fancy way of saying, "we build stuff"). But wait, there's more! With over $2 billion ushered in over a mere seven years and $500 million in contracts just two years in, it's safe to say you're not just playing Monopoly in your spare time. You've got real-world experience—and apparently, a knack for collecting accolades like they're Pokémon cards.

Now, let's talk about the grand tapestry of diversity that comes wrapped in these seven companies. For those keeping score, we've got defense, tech, healthcare, and construction—just your average Tuesday in the life of a modern-day mogul.

And what's your strategy, you ask? If you don't know how to navigate these industries, just buy one! It's like shopping for shoes, but with slightly higher stakes and a lot more paperwork. Let's not forget the classic 80's anthem "Opportunities" by the Pet Shop Boys—your personal theme song for the entrepreneurial journey. "I've got the brains, you've got the looks," indeed!

If anyone has the brawn but can't quite figure out which way is up in the defense sector, feel free to slide into my DMs. After all, partnerships are like a well-rehearsed dance—one leads, the other follows, and both of us hopefully end up with some sweet profits.

And let's be real: just like The Police, every move you make, every breath you take is not just a strategic business decision but also a pathway to success and a leveling up to that generous side of you. Picture Goku from Dragon Ball Z powering up! For me, I love stacking the cash to fund the charity work that warms my heart, and I hope you'll do the same. And if you want to partner with me, it's a requirement. It's practically a win-win—more money in your pocket means more good in the world. Who knew capitalism could come with a side of compassion? So, buckle up, dear entrepreneurs; this ride is about to get bumpy and, dare I say, enlightening! Let's raise a glass to opportunity—because in the government world, it seems to be the gift that keeps on giving!

# Introduction to Federal Contracting

## Introduction: Where Dreams Go to Die and Wallets Go to Fatten

Alright, let's dive into the thrilling world of federal contracting. Buckle up because this ride is about as exciting as watching paint dry on a government building – but hey, at least that paint's worth millions.

## When: The Current Cesspool of Bureaucratic Bliss

Picture this: a vast landscape of paperwork, red tape, and enough acronyms to make your head spin faster than the Tasmanian Devil on a caffeine binge. Welcome to the current state of federal contracting, a booming industry that's growing faster than Kylie Jenner's Instagram following. It's a world where the government throws money around like Tony Stark at a charity gala – except with less style and more questionable decision-making.

Example: As of 2023, federal contracting reached over $600 billion, with agencies like the Department of Defense leading the pack. For emerging businesses, this represents a treasure trove of opportunities ripe for the picking.

"In the middle of difficulty lies opportunity." – Albert Einstein

**Reflective Questions:**

- How do you perceive the current landscape of federal contracting?

- What excites you (or intimidates you) most about entering this field?

---

# Why: Because Who Doesn't Want a Slice of Uncle Sam's Pie?

Understanding the importance of federal contracts is like grasping why the Kardashians are famous – it defies logic, but it's undeniably significant. For businesses, it's the golden ticket to Willy Wonka's chocolate factory, except instead of candy, you're swimming in a river of steady cash flow. For the economy, it's the vibranium injection keeping those GDP muscles as flexed as Captain America's biceps. So strap in because we're about to explore why everybody and their corporate cousin is clamoring for a piece of this bureaucratic banquet like it's the last slice of pizza at a frat party.

**Example:** Companies like Lockheed Martin and Boeing thrive on federal contracts, showcasing how lucrative and vital these partnerships can be for business growth and sustainability.

"Success usually comes to those who are too busy to be looking for it." – Henry David Thoreau.

**Reflective Questions:**

- What do you think are the primary motivations for businesses to pursue federal contracts?

- How do you believe federal contracts contribute to the overall economy?

---

# How: A Step-by-Step Guide to Selling Your Soul (and Services) to the Government

1. Drown yourself in paperwork like you're Jack at the end of Titanic – but with less romance and more frustration.

2. Learn a new language called "Government Speak" that makes Klingon seem straightforward.

3. Navigate a labyrinth of regulations so complex that it makes The Maze Runner look like a kiddie playground.

4. Sacrifice your firstborn to the altar of compliance (or at least your sanity and social life).

5. Voila! You're now a federal contractor (maybe) – congratulations on completing your transformation into a suit-wearing, acronym-spewing bureaucratic zombie.

**Example:** For instance, the requirement for a DUNS number or registration in the System for Award Management (SAM) can feel overwhelming, but these are necessary steps for entering the market.

"The future belongs to those who believe in the beauty of their dreams." – Eleanor Roosevelt.

### Reflective Questions:

- Which part of the contracting process do you think will be the most daunting for you?

- How can you prepare yourself to handle the complexities of government regulations?

---

# The Four Most Profitable Sectors in Government Contracting: A Snarky Guide to Cashing In

Welcome to the wild world of government contracting, where the only thing more exciting than the prospect of landing a contract is the sheer amount of paperwork you'll have to fill out! Some sectors are hotter than a summer day in Phoenix, driven by the ever-growing demand for products and services that keep Uncle Sam happy. So, grab your notepad (or your favorite snack), and let's dive into the four most profitable sectors in government contracting—because who doesn't want to make a boatload of cash while navigating bureaucracy?

Let's break down the top four categories for federal contracting in the United States, where the government spends its cash like a kid in a candy store. And just to spice things up, I'll throw in the market share percentages because who doesn't love a little data?

## Overview of the Top 4 Markets

1. Defense and Aerospace (40%): Welcome to the big leagues, where contracts are all about military might and high-flying tech. This category is where the government gets its shiny new toys— think fighter jets, advanced weapon systems, and all the military tech that would make even Tony Stark a little jealous. Companies here often cozy up to the Department of Defense like it's a high-stakes game of poker, and they know how to play their cards right.

2. Information Technology (IT) (30%): In the IT arena, the government is pouring money into everything from software development to cybersecurity—because who doesn't want to keep the hackers at bay? As agencies scramble to modernize their tech faster than you can say cloud computing, this sector is booming like a blockbuster movie franchise. If you can code, secure, or optimize, you're golden!

3. Construction and Infrastructure (20%): Grab your hard hats, folks! This category is all about building and maintaining the nation's physical backbone—federal buildings, military bases, and everything in between. From renovation to brand-new constructions, these contracts are crucial for keeping the American dream standing tall and proud. Think of it as the government's way of saying, We need more than just a roof over our heads.

4. Health and Human Services (10%): Last but not least, we have the health sector, where contractors are responsible for everything from medical supplies to public health initiatives. Working with the Department of Health and Human Services, these companies are the unsung heroes trying to keep the populace healthy and happy. After all, who doesn't want to make a difference while cashing in on government contracts?

These categories represent the diverse needs of Uncle Sam and offer a buffet of opportunities for contractors across the board. So, whether you're building the next big thing, securing data like a digital fortress, or keeping our troops equipped, the federal contracting world is ripe for the picking!

# 1. Defense

Welcome to the wild and wacky world of defense contracting, where the government spends more cash on weapons and military tech than a kid blows on Fortnite skins. We're talking about contracts for everything from shiny new fighter jets that could make Iron Man jealous to cutting-edge cybersecurity solutions that keep hackers at bay like a superhero's force field. With global tensions rising faster than a Netflix binge-watch list, funding in this sector is as robust as Thor's biceps—seriously, it's a goldmine!

If you're in aerospace, defense tech, or surveillance systems, congratulations! You're sitting on a treasure trove, and the U.S. Department of Defense is like that rich uncle who can't stop showering cash on his favorite nephews and nieces. Guess what? That could be you! Lockheed Martin and Northrop Grumman are practically the Avengers of this sector, providing advanced tech and support services that keep our nation safe. Want to play in the big leagues? This is your calling!

In war, there are no unwounded soldiers – José Narosky.

Now, let's glide into the IT sector, where the government spends more on tech than Tony Stark does on new suits. This arena encompasses everything from software development to cloud computing, and let's not forget the sweet, sweet cybersecurity solutions that keep the digital villains at bay. As agencies modernize their tech like they're on a reality show makeover, the demand for IT services is skyrocketing.

With the feds dropping billions on IT services annually, if you're the kind of whiz who can whip up a foolproof cybersecurity plan or manage a massive database, brace yourself for a treasure trove of contracts waiting just for you. Companies like IBM and Cisco are rocking the government contracting scene, providing the tech solutions that keep agencies running smoother than a well-oiled machine.

The future is already here – it's just not evenly distributed – William Gibson.

Now, let's dive into the nitty-gritty of defense contracts. The choice of a specific type of defense contract isn't just a game of chance; it's influenced by several factors that would make even the most seasoned poker player sweat.

First off, consider the nature of the work. If the project is as clear as a well-written script, fixed-price contracts are the way to go. But when the work is as uncertain as a plot twist in a Christopher Nolan movie, cost-plus contracts might be more suitable.

Then there's risk allocation—a fancy term for figuring out who's holding the bag when things go south. Fixed-price contracts slap the risk onto the contractor, while cost-plus contracts shift it to the government. It's like a game of hot potato: who wants to catch the risk?

Cost certainty also plays a crucial role. If the government needs predictability, they'll lean towards fixed-price contracts; however, if costs are as unpredictable as weather forecasts in April, cost-plus or time-and-materials contracts might fit the bill.

And let's not forget about the duration of the project. Long-term projects with changing requirements might benefit from flexible contract types like IDIQ (Indefinite Delivery/Indefinite Quantity) or time-and-materials contracts. These contracts are like a buffet—there's something for everyone!

Market conditions can also sway contract choices. In a competitive market, fixed-price contracts might be the norm, while niche markets can lead to cost-plus contracts to attract bidders.

Past performance is a big deal, too. If a contractor has a solid track record, they might find themselves getting the same type of contracts again and again, like an artist getting booked for the same festival. Talk about a sweet gig!

Regulatory requirements and funding availability can dictate contract types, too. If funding is tighter than a drum, fixed-price contracts may be favored to control costs. But when cash is flowing, the government might be more flexible.

Control and oversight needs come into play as well. Projects requiring close monitoring may benefit from cost-plus or time-and-materials contracts, where ongoing assessments are necessary—think of it as keeping a watchful eye on your favorite sports team.

Let's not overlook the type of deliverables as well, whether it's goods, services, or a combination, which influences which contract type is the best fit. For example, service contracts or R&D contracts may require different arrangements compared to production contracts for tangible goods.

And if the project scope is likely to change, the government might prefer flexible contracts, like IDIQ or time-and-materials contracts. They're like the yoga pants of contracts—flexible and ready for anything!

Finally, small business considerations come into play. The

government often sets aside contracts for small businesses, which can influence the selection of contract types tailored to encourage participation from smaller contractors.

So, what types of contracts are we looking at? Here's the lowdown:

1. Fixed-Price Contracts: Set prices for goods or services, no matter what. Perfect for well-defined projects.

2. Cost-Plus Contracts: Pay for all allowable costs plus a profit. Great for uncertain projects.

3. Time-and-Materials Contracts: Reimburse for actual costs of labor and materials. Ideal for undefined scopes.

4. Indefinite Delivery/Indefinite Quantity (IDIQ) Contracts: Flexibility is key with these contracts, allowing for indefinite supplies or services.

5. Basic Ordering Agreements (BOAs): Set the stage for future contracts, simplifying recurring needs.

6. Small Business Contracts: Tailored for small businesses, promoting their participation.

7. Service Contracts: Focus on services rather than goods—think maintenance and consulting.

8. Research and Development (R&D) Contracts: Fund innovation in defense capabilities.

9. Foreign Military Sales (FMS): Sell defense equipment to foreign governments—because why not?

10. Production Contracts: Ensure timely delivery of defense systems and equipment.

11. Logistics and Support Contracts: Provide essential logistics support for defense systems.

12. Construction Contracts: For the building and renovation of military facilities.

Now, let's talk about how the federal government evaluates the performance of defense contractors. The evaluation process is as rigorous as a superhero training montage. Contractors are assessed based on several key criteria:

1. Cost Control: Are contractors able to deliver their goods and services within budget? If costs spiral out of control, it's like a budget-busting blockbuster movie.

2. Schedule Adherence: Timeliness is crucial. If a contractor misses deadlines, it's akin to showing up late to the superhero showdown—nobody likes a tardy hero.

3. Quality of Work: The products and services provided must meet or exceed specified standards. Think of it as ensuring that the gadgets are as reliable as Batman's utility belt.

4. Past Performance: A contractor's history with previous contracts is a good predictor of future performance. If they've successfully saved the day before, they're likely to do it again.

5. Customer Satisfaction: Feedback from the government agencies using the services plays a critical role. Positive reviews are like five-star ratings on a popular streaming service.

6. Compliance with Regulations: Contractors must adhere to federal regulations and guidelines. Non-compliance is like breaking

the rules of the superhero code—there are consequences.

7. Innovation and Technology: The ability to provide innovative solutions and cutting-edge technology can set a contractor apart. Think of it as having the most advanced gadgets in your arsenal.

Now, if you're looking to partner with the big guns in this sector, here's a list of some of the top defense companies that are prominent in federal government contracting:

1. Lockheed Martin - www.lockheedmartin.com
2. Northrop Grumman - www.northropgrumman.com
3. Raytheon Technologies - www.rtx.com
4. Boeing - www.boeing.com
5. General Dynamics - www.gd.com
6. BAE Systems - www.baesystems.com
7. Hewlett Packard Enterprise (HPE) - www.hpe.com
8. L3Harris Technologies - www.l3harris.com
9. Thales Group - www.thalesgroup.com
10. Leonardo - www.leonardocompany.com
11. SAIC - www.saic.com
12. ManTech International - www.mantech.com
13. General Atomics - www.ga.com
14. Textron - www.textron.com
15. HII (Huntington Ingalls Industries) www.huntingtoningalls.com
16. KBR, Inc. - www.kbr.com
17. DynCorp International - www.dyn-intl.com
18. FLIR Systems - www.flir.com
19. Sierra Nevada Corporation - www.sncorp.com
20. AeroVironment - www.aerovironment.com
21. Rockwell Collins - www.collinsaerospace.com
22. Ceradyne - www.ceradyne.com

23. Rheinmetall AG - www.rheinmetall.com
24. Viasat - www.viasat.com
25. Palantir Technologies - www.palantir.com
26. Cubic Corporation - www.cubic.com
27. Battelle Memorial Institute - www.battelle.org
28. Peraton - www.peraton.com
29. Amentum - www.amentum.com
30. Parker Hannifin - www.parker.com
31. Teledyne Technologies - www.teledyne.com
32. Sikorsky Aircraft www.lockheedmartin.com/en-us/products/sikorsky.html
33. Elbit Systems - www.elbitsystems.com
34. Deloitte Consulting - www2.deloitte.com/us/en/pages/consulting/solutions/government-services.html
35. McKinsey & Company - www.mckinsey.com
36. Accenture - www.accenture.com
37. CGI Group - www.cgi.com
38. Bain & Company - www.bain.com
39. Boston Consulting Group (BCG) - www.bcg.com
40. AT&T Government Solutions www.business.att.com/solutions/government/
41. Cisco Systems - www.cisco.com/go/government

These companies are well-established in the defense sector and often engage in federal government contracting, providing a variety of services and products. If you're looking to partner with any of them, visiting their websites will give you insights into their capabilities and contracting opportunities.

So, gear up! The defense contracting world is waiting for you, and it's time to make your mark in this high-sta Defense.

## 2. Information Technology

Welcome to the dazzling world of the IT sector, where the government spends more on technology than Tony Stark spends on his latest suits. This sector spans everything from software development to cloud computing, with a hefty dose of cybersecurity solutions to keep those pesky hackers at bay. As agencies modernize their tech like they're on a reality show makeover, the demand for IT services is skyrocketing.

When it comes to the types of contracts utilized in the IT space, cost-plus contracts and fixed-price contracts are the heavy hitters. Cost-plus contracts are favored for projects where the scope can change or is initially unclear, allowing for flexibility in funding. For instance, the Department of Defense often uses these contracts for innovative tech projects where requirements may evolve. On the other hand, fixed-price contracts are the go-to for well-defined projects with predictable costs. An example can be seen in software development projects where the specifications are clear from the outset.

The impact of computing services on government operations cannot be overstated. With the feds dropping billions on IT services annually, these technologies streamline processes, enhance security, and improve data management—keeping the gears of government running smoother than a well-oiled machine. For example, IBM provides cloud solutions that help agencies manage vast amounts of data efficiently, while Cisco's cybersecurity tools protect sensitive information across federal networks.

So, which departments are the biggest consumers of IT resources? The Department of Defense takes the lead due to its extensive reliance on advanced technology for operations and security. Following closely are the Department of Homeland Security, which focuses on cybersecurity and infrastructure protection, and the Department of Health and Human Services, which uses IT for health data management and public health initiatives. These departments offer a wealth of contracts, making them prime targets for IT contractors. For instance, the DHS has awarded contracts to companies like Northrop Grumman for cybersecurity solutions, while HHS partners with companies like Leidos for health data management solutions.

For new businesses looking to break into the IT federal

contracting market, it can feel like entering a high-stakes poker game. Here are some steps to consider:

1. Understand the Market: Research the specific needs of federal agencies and identify where your services can fit in. For example, if you specialize in cybersecurity, target agencies focusing on national security.

2. Register on SAM: Ensure you are registered on the System for Award Management (SAM) to be eligible for government contracts.

3. Network: Attend industry conferences, participate in forums, and connect with established contractors to learn the ropes. Building relationships can lead to partnership opportunities.

4. Start Small: Consider pursuing smaller contracts or teaming up with larger contractors to gain experience and credibility. For instance, you might partner with a company like Accenture to bid on a larger project.

Now, let's reflect on this journey. What unique services can your business offer that sets you apart from competitors? How can you leverage partnerships to enhance your capabilities? And ultimately, what is your long-term vision for sustaining growth in the federal IT contracting space?

With the right strategy and a sprinkle of determination, the federal IT contracting world is ripe for the picking! Companies like Amazon Web Services, Microsoft, and Oracle are leading the charge, providing a wide range of services that keep the federal government's IT landscape robust and efficient.

Here's a quick look at some of the top IT contractors in the federal government:

1. Amazon Web Services (AWS)

Website: www.aws.amazon.com

2. Microsoft Corporation

Website: www.microsoft.com

3. IBM Corporation

Website: www.ibm.com

4. Oracle Corporation

Website: www.oracle.com

5. Dell Technologies

Website: www.dell.com

6. Cisco Systems, Inc.

Website: www.cisco.com

7. Hewlett Packard Enterprise (HPE)

Website: www.hpe.com

8. Northrop Grumman Corporation

Website: www.northropgrumman.com

9. General Dynamics Information Technology (GDIT)

Website: www.gdit.com

10. SAIC

Website: www.saic.com

11. Raytheon Technologies

Website: www.rtx.com

12. Leidos

Website: www.leidos.com

13. Boeing

Website: www.boeing.com

14. L3Harris Technologies

Website: www.l3harris.com

15. CGI Group

Website: www.cgi.com

16. ManTech International

Website: www.mantech.com

17. Accenture

Website: www.accenture.com

18. Palantir Technologies

Website: www.palantir.com

19. KBR, Inc.

Website: www.kbr.com

20. Motorola Solutions

Website: www.motorolasolutions.com

21. Veritas Technologies

Website: www.veritas.com

22. VMware

Website: www.vmware.com

23. Splunk Inc.

Website: www.splunk.com

24. ServiceNow

Website: www.servicenow.com

25. Salesforce

Website: www.salesforce.com

26. Qualys

Website: www.qualys.com

27. FireEye

Website: www.fireeye.com

28. DigitalGlobe (now part of Maxar Technologies)

Website: www.maxar.com

29. Epic Systems Corporation

Website: www.epic.com

30. Red Hat

Website: www.redhat.com

31. SAS Institute

Website: www.sas.com

32. Fujitsu

Website: www.fujitsu.com

33. Cisco Meraki

Website: meraki.cisco.com

34. AeroVironment

Website: www.aerovironment.com

35. Tata Consultancy Services (TCS)

Website: www.tcs.com

36. Capgemini

Website: www.capgemini.com

37. Bain & Company

Website: www.bain.com

38. Boston Consulting Group (BCG)

Website: www.bcg.com

39. McKinsey & Company

Website: www.mckinsey.com

40. Deloitte Consulting

Website:
www2.deloitte.com/us/en/pages/consulting/solutions/government-services.html

41. KPMG

Website: home.kpmg/us/en/home.html

42. GDIT (General Dynamics Information Technology)

Website: www.gdit.com

43. Hewlett Packard Enterprise (HPE)

Website: www.hpe.com

44. Cognizant Technology Solutions

Website: www.cognizant.com

45. Infor

Website: www.infor.com

46. Sierra Nevada Corporation

Website: www.sncorp.com

47. Unisys Corporation

Website: www.unisys.com

48. Zebra Technologies

Website: www.zebra.com

49. Palo Alto Networks

Website: www.paloaltonetworks.com

50. Atlassian

Website: www.atlassian.com

These companies are prominent players in the federal government's Information Technology contracting landscape, providing a wide range of services and solutions. With the right approach and innovative ideas, new businesses can carve out their niche in this thriving market.

Small businesses looking to navigate federal contracting regulations have access to a variety of resources designed to provide guidance and education. Here are some key resources:

1. Small Business Administration (SBA): The SBA offers numerous resources, including training programs, workshops, and guides specifically focused on federal contracting. Their website provides information on how to obtain government contracts, understand regulations, and explore available funding options.

2. Federal Acquisition Regulation (FAR): The FAR is the primary regulation governing federal procurement. Small businesses can access the FAR online to familiarize themselves with the rules and procedures that govern federal contracting.

3. SBA's 8(a) Business Development Program: This program helps small businesses gain access to federal contracting opportunities and guides regulations and requirements.

4. Procurement Technical Assistance Centers (PTACs): PTACs offer free or low-cost assistance to small businesses seeking to understand and compete for government contracts. They provide training, one-on-one counseling, and resources on the bidding process and compliance requirements.

5. The General Services Administration (GSA): The GSA provides resources and tools for small businesses, including information on how to obtain GSA schedules, which can simplify the contracting process with federal agencies.

6. Government Contracting Associations: Organizations such as the National 8(a) Association and the Association of Procurement Technical Assistance Centers provide networking opportunities, training, and resources to help small businesses understand federal contracting.

7. Webinars and Online Training: Many organizations, including the SBA and PTACs, offer free webinars and online training sessions covering various aspects of federal contracting, including compliance and regulations.

8. Local Small Business Development Centers (SBDCs): SBDCs provide personalized assistance to small businesses, including help with understanding federal contracts and navigating regulations.

9. Federal Agency Resources: Many federal agencies have their own small business offices that provide resources, training, and guidance tailored to their specific contracting processes. Checking the websites of agencies relevant to your industry can be beneficial.

10. Online Forums and Communities: Platforms like LinkedIn and industry-specific forums allow small business owners to connect, share experiences, and seek advice on federal contracting.

Utilizing these resources can help small businesses build a solid understanding of federal contracting regulations, increasing their chances of successfully securing government contracts.

Here are some reflective questions based on the provided text about the IT sector in federal contracting:

1. Understanding Your Unique Value: What unique services or solutions does your business offer that differentiate you from established competitors in the IT contracting space?

2. Identifying Target Agencies: Which specific federal agencies are most aligned with your business's capabilities, and how can you tailor your offerings to meet their unique needs?

3. Adapting to Contract Types: How can you effectively navigate the complexities of cost-plus and fixed-price contracts to maximize your chances of securing government contracts?

4. Networking Strategies: What strategies can you implement to build meaningful relationships with other contractors and government officials that will enhance your visibility in the federal contracting arena?

5. Market Research: How can you conduct thorough market research to understand better current trends and demands within the federal IT sector?

6. Leveraging Technology: In what ways can technology (e.g., cloud solutions cybersecurity tools) be integrated into your offerings to provide additional value to government agencies?

7. Partnership Opportunities: What potential partnership opportunities exist with larger contractors that could help your business gain credibility and experience in federal contracting?

8. Long-Term Growth Vision: What is your long-term vision for growth in the federal IT contracting market, and what milestones do you aim to achieve in the next few years?

9. Learning from Established Players: How can you learn from the strategies and successes of leading IT contractors, such as IBM or Amazon Web Services, to inform your own approach?

10. Risk Management: How will you manage the risks associated with federal contracting, especially in terms of project scope changes and funding fluctuations?

These reflective questions encourage critical thinking on successfully navigating the federal IT contracting landscape and identifying opportunities for growth and success.

# 3. Healthcare

Winning federal contracts in the healthcare sector is like trying to solve a Rubik's Cube blindfolded—challenging but not impossible if you know a few tricks. Here's the lowdown on how companies typically pull off this magic act, sprinkled with real-world examples to keep things lively.

First off, companies dive headfirst into understanding the market. They research the federal healthcare landscape to pinpoint which agencies need their services. As the saying goes, "Knowledge is power," and knowing the players can make all the difference. For instance, if a company realizes that the Department of Veterans Affairs is ramping up telehealth services, it can tailor their offerings to fit that need. It's like being the first to know about a new iPhone launch; you want to be ready when the demand hits.

Next up, registration and compliance are non-negotiables. Firms must register in the System for Award Management (SAM) and ensure they have all necessary certifications. Think of it as getting your VIP pass to the government contracting party; without it, you're stuck outside, watching the fun unfold from a distance like a kid outside a candy store.

Building relationships is also key. Companies schmooze at industry conferences, workshops, and government events, hoping to connect with decision-makers and other contractors. These connections can lead to valuable partnerships and insider tips. For example, a small tech firm might team up with a larger contractor to tackle a massive healthcare IT project, boosting its credibility and chances of success. It's like finding your business soulmate at a networking event—together, you can conquer the world.

When it comes to responding to Requests for Proposals (RFPs), companies keep their eyes peeled for opportunities. Crafting compelling proposals that clearly outline how they can meet the government's needs and provide value is essential. Think of it as dating—if you don't impress on the first date, there won't be a second. Just ask the company that lost a contract because their proposal reads like a grocery list instead of a passionate love letter. "You had me at hello" only works if the hello is actually impressive.

Leveraging past performance is another ace up their sleeve. Demonstrating a track record of success in similar projects can significantly enhance credibility. Federal agencies love to see that a contractor has been there, done that, and got the T-shirt. McKesson, for example, has a long history of supplying essential healthcare products to government agencies, making them a go-to choice. If you've got the experience, flaunt it like a trophy.

Utilizing set-aside programs is a golden ticket for many companies. Many federal contracts are reserved for small businesses, minority-owned businesses, and other specific categories. If a company can qualify for these programs, it's like having a secret menu at an exclusive restaurant—only a select few gets to enjoy it. The 8(a) Business Development Program is a prime example, helping disadvantaged businesses access federal contracting opportunities.

Pricing strategies matter, too. It's not just about being the cheapest on the block; companies must strike a balance between competitive pricing and the ability to deliver quality services. No one wants to be the contractor that cuts corners just to save a buck. Remember the company that won a contract by offering a rock-bottom price but ended up turning in shoddy work? Yeah, they're not getting invited back. "You get what you pay for" is a lesson learned the hard way.

Partnerships and joint ventures can also bolster a company's capabilities. By teaming up with other businesses, they can increase their chances of winning contracts, especially for larger projects. It's like forming a superhero alliance—together, they can take on bigger foes. Think of how Siemens Healthineers collaborates with smaller firms to enhance their technology offerings.

Finally, staying informed is crucial. The federal contracting landscape is constantly evolving, and companies that keep up with policies, regulations, and market trends will always have a leg up on the competition. For instance, knowing when new funding is available for health IT projects can give a company the edge in securing contracts. "With great power comes great responsibility," and staying informed is part of that responsibility.

For small businesses trying to qualify for set-aside programs, the road can be bumpy. They often face a maze of eligibility requirements that can change faster than you can say "government bureaucracy." Many struggle to navigate the certification processes, which can feel like jumping through hoops while blindfolded.

Then there's the registration in SAM, which can be as confusing as assembling IKEA furniture without the manual. Small businesses might find themselves stuck in a cycle of delays and incomplete applications. Limited resources are another hurdle. Many small businesses operate with a skeleton crew and tight budgets, making it tough to dedicate time to navigating the federal contracting labyrinth.

Responding to RFPs can also feel like deciphering an ancient language. The complex proposal requirements can overwhelm small businesses, especially if they lack experience in federal contracting. Competing against larger firms with established relationships and extensive resources can feel like bringing a knife to a gunfight. As they say in "The Hunger Games," may the odds be ever in your favor.

The administrative burden of compliance and reporting can weigh heavily on small businesses, diverting their focus from actually running their operations. Plus, finding the right information about contracts and set-aside programs can sometimes feel like searching for a needle in a haystack. Networking limitations can restrict small businesses' access to valuable insights and partnerships. And let's not forget the financial constraints; pursuing federal contracts can be pricey, and limited access to capital can deter small businesses from fully engaging in the process.

By being aware of these challenges and seeking out resources and support, small businesses can better navigate the federal contracting landscape and increase their chances of qualifying for set-aside programs. After all, knowledge is power, and a little savvy goes a long way in this game.

Now, let's talk about certifications. When it comes to federal contracting in the healthcare sector, several certifications can make or break a company's chances of success:

1. Small Business Administration (SBA) Certifications: To qualify as a small business for federal contracts, companies often need to meet the SBA's size standards based on industry-specific

metrics. This certification is essential for accessing set-aside programs.

2. 8(a) Business Development Program: This SBA program helps small disadvantaged businesses gain access to federal contracting opportunities. Companies must apply and demonstrate social and economic disadvantage to qualify.

3. Women-Owned Small Business (WOSB) Certification: This certification allows women-owned businesses to participate in federal contracting opportunities specifically set aside for them. The process involves demonstrating that the business is at least 51% owned and controlled by women.

4. Economically Disadvantaged Women-Owned Small Business (EDWOSB) Certification: Similar to the WOSB certification, this one requires businesses to prove economic disadvantage, providing additional opportunities for women entrepreneurs.

5. Minority-Owned Business Certification: Various organizations, including the National Minority Supplier Development Council (NMSDC), offer certifications for minority-owned businesses. This certification can help businesses access federal contracts set aside for minority-owned firms.

6. Veteran-Owned Small Business (VOSB) Certification: This certification is for businesses that are at least 51% owned and controlled by veterans, opening doors to federal contracting opportunities specifically aimed at veteran-owned businesses.

7. Service-Disabled Veteran-Owned Small Business (SDVOSB) Certification: This subset of VOSB certification is for businesses owned by service-disabled veterans, providing access to set-aside contracts and giving companies a competitive edge.

8. HUBZone Certification: The Historically Underutilized Business Zone (HUBZone) program encourages economic development in specific areas. Businesses must meet location requirements and demonstrate that they employ residents from HUBZone areas to qualify.

9. ISO Certifications: While not specific to federal contracting, certifications like ISO 9001 (Quality Management) and ISO 13485 (Medical Devices) can enhance credibility in the healthcare sector, signaling a commitment to quality.

10. HIPAA Compliance: For healthcare-related contracts, demonstrating compliance with the Health Insurance Portability and Accountability Act (HIPAA) is crucial. This involves protecting patient information and ensuring data privacy, often a requirement in federal contracts.

By obtaining these certifications, companies can enhance their credibility, gain access to valuable contracting opportunities, and ultimately increase their chances of success in the competitive federal healthcare sector. Ready to dive into the world of healthcare companies hunting for small and minority business partners? Buckle up because this adventure is just getting started!

1. Market Understanding: How well do I understand the federal healthcare landscape? What specific agencies or needs have I identified that align with my company's services?

2. Research Strategies: What methods do I currently used to gather information about federal healthcare contracts? How can I improve my research strategies to anticipate market demands better?

3. Registration and Compliance: Am I fully aware of the

registration requirements in the System for Award Management (SAM)? How can I streamline the registration process to ensure compliance and avoid delays?

4. Building Relationships: How effective am I at networking within the healthcare contracting space? What steps can I take to deepen my connections with decision-makers and other contractors?

5. Proposal Development: How do I approach crafting proposals for Requests for Proposals (RFPs)? Am I ensuring that my proposals are compelling and tailored to meet the specific needs of the government?

6. Leveraging Past Performance: How do I showcase my company's past performance and successes in healthcare projects? Am I effectively communicating my experience to enhance my credibility with potential clients?

7. Utilizing Set-Aside Programs: Have I explored the various set-aside programs available to my business? What certifications or qualifications do I need to pursue to take full advantage of these opportunities?

8. Pricing Strategies: How do I determine my pricing for federal contracts? Am I balancing competitive pricing with the need to maintain quality and sustainability in my services?

9. Partnerships and Collaborations: What potential partnerships can I explore within the healthcare sector? How can I identify companies that align with my business goals for joint ventures?

10. Staying Informed: How do I keep myself updated with the latest policies, regulations, and trends in federal healthcare contracting? What resources can I leverage to enhance my

knowledge and adaptability?

11. Navigating Challenges: What specific hurdles have I encountered in pursuing federal contracts in the healthcare sector? How can I develop strategies to overcome these challenges?

12. Understanding Eligibility Requirements: Am I familiar with the eligibility requirements for various certifications in the healthcare contracting sector? How can I ensure that my business meets these criteria?

13. Administrative Burdens: How do I manage the administrative aspects of compliance and reporting? Am I dedicating sufficient resources to ensure that these tasks do not detract from my core business operations?

14. Financial Planning: How do I approach financial planning for pursuing federal contracts? Am I aware of the costs involved and how to secure funding to support my initiatives?

15. Reflecting on Success: How do I define success in the context of federal healthcare contracting? Am I focusing solely on financial metrics, or do I also consider the impact of my work on the healthcare community?

# 4. Construction and Infrastructure: A Dynamic Sector

The construction and infrastructure sector is akin to that dependable, albeit slightly scruffy, friend who always needs a ride—perennially in demand and often facing challenges. This sector encompasses contracts for building, renovating, and maintaining everything from government facilities to roads and bridges. With the U.S. infrastructure resembling something out of a horror movie, the government is currently showering funds like confetti, thanks to initiatives like the Infrastructure Investment and Jobs Act. "If you build it, they will come," echoes the sentiment that investing in infrastructure paves the way for economic growth and community development.

## Opportunities Abound

For contractors skilled in construction, engineering, and project management, this is a golden age reminiscent of a buffet brimming with opportunities. Major firms like Bechtel and Kiewit are the Usain Bolt of the industry, racing ahead by securing substantial government contracts and capitalizing on the infrastructure boom. Their efforts are vital in ensuring that the roads we travel and the buildings we work in are safe and reliable.

## The Transformative Role of AI

Artificial intelligence (AI) is revolutionizing project management in construction by utilizing data analysis, machine learning, and predictive modeling. Here's how AI is changing the game:

1. Data Analysis and Insights: AI sifts through vast amounts of historical project data—think of it as the Sherlock Holmes of construction—finding patterns that help predict future outcomes.

2. Risk Assessment: Much like the Avengers assessing threats, AI evaluates potential risks by analyzing factors like site conditions and workforce performance, enabling proactive measures.

3. Schedule Optimization: AI can optimize project schedules by determining the most efficient task sequences, ensuring deadlines are met with precision akin to a well-timed movie release.

4. Cost Prediction: Just as Marty McFly used his time machine to predict outcomes, machine learning models analyze past costs to forecast future expenses, helping to keep budgets in check.

5. Performance Monitoring: AI continually tracks project performance, allowing managers to make real-time adjustments and stay on course, akin to GPS recalculating routes.

6. Resource Allocation: By predicting required resources, AI ensures that the right amount of labor and materials are available when needed, reducing downtime and enhancing efficiency.

7. Enhanced Communication: AI-driven tools improve communication among stakeholders, providing real-time data visualization that keeps everyone informed—a necessity in any successful collaboration.

8. Change Impact Analysis: AI assesses the implications of project changes, enabling informed decisions just like how superheroes strategize before a big battle.

9. Quality Control: By predicting quality issues before they arise, AI helps maintain standards, minimizing rework and ensuring projects are up to snuff.

10. Continuous Improvement: AI systems learn and evolve over time, enhancing their predictive capabilities much like characters growing throughout a series.

### Technologies Shaping the Future

Several cutting-edge technologies are enhancing construction practices, including:

-Building Information Modeling (BIM): This digital representation of a building enhances collaboration and project management, allowing teams to visualize projects before they break ground.

- Drones: Used for site surveys and inspections, drones provide real-time data and aerial imagery, transforming how construction companies collect and analyze information.

- 3D Printing: This technology is revolutionizing the fabrication of building components, allowing for rapid prototyping and customization, much like how Tony Stark builds his suits.

- Augmented and Virtual Reality (AR/VR): These technologies are used for design visualization and training, engaging stakeholders, and helping identify potential design flaws before construction begins.

- Internet of Things (IoT): IoT devices monitor conditions on job sites, enhancing safety and providing real-time data on equipment and workforce performance.

- Robotics and Automation: From bricklaying to demolition, robotics are taking on dangerous tasks, improving precision and reducing labor costs.

- Prefabrication and Modular Construction: These methods lead to faster construction times and reduced waste, showing that efficiency can indeed be stylish.

- Smart Wearables: Devices like smart helmets monitor worker safety conditions, ensuring compliance and enhancing on-site safety.

**The Importance of Supplier Diversity**

Supplier diversity plays a pivotal role in sustainability assessments. Engaging diverse suppliers fosters creativity and opens new avenues for innovative solutions. Supporting underrepresented communities aligns with sustainability goals by promoting equity and resilience. "Diversity is not a reason to be proud; it's a reason to be successful," and companies embracing this principle often enjoy enhanced reputations and stakeholder trust.

**Assessing Sustainability Practices**

To assess the sustainability practices of potential suppliers, companies often utilize various methods:

1. Surveys and Questionnaires: Gathering detailed information on energy use and waste management.

2. Certifications: Looking for recognized certifications like ISO 14001 or LEED to gauge a supplier's commitment to sustainability.

3. Audits: Conducting on-site assessments to evaluate environmental practices.

4. Performance Metrics: Establishing KPIs to track sustainability efforts, such as carbon footprint and recycling rates.

5. Sustainability Reports: Requesting detailed reports that outline practices and progress.

6. Collaboration: Engaging in discussions with suppliers to understand their sustainability initiatives better.

## Selecting Suppliers for Federal Contracts

When it comes to selecting construction companies for federal contracts, several factors come into play:

1. Experience and Past Performance: A proven track record of successfully completing similar projects is crucial.

2. Technical Capability: The expertise and resources available to meet project requirements.

3. Financial Stability: Evaluating financial health ensures the company can handle large-scale projects.

4. Compliance with Regulations: A history of adhering to federal regulations is vital.

5. Cost Structure: Competitive pricing must balance quality and value.

6. Project Management: Effective planning and communication strategies are essential for successful project execution.

Notable Organizations to Join

For construction companies involved in federal contracting, joining industry organizations can provide valuable resources and networking opportunities. Some notable organizations include:

- Associated General Contractors of America (AGC): [www.agc.org](https://www.agc.org)

- National Association of General Contractors (NAGC):

[www.nagc.org](https://www.nagc.org)

- American Society of Civil Engineers (ASCE): [www.asce.org](https://www.asce.org)

## Conclusion

The construction industry is at the nexus of innovation and opportunity, driven by advanced technologies and a commitment to sustainability. As we embrace these changes, it's crucial to remember that "Success is the sum of small efforts, repeated day in and day out." By fostering diversity, leveraging AI, and adopting cutting-edge technologies, construction companies can not only meet the demands of today but also lay the groundwork for a more sustainable and resilient future. In the words of the great Bob the Builder, "Can We Fix It? Yes, we can!"

Here are some reflective questions based on the text provided:

## Reflective Questions

1. Understanding the Sector: How does the analogy of the construction sector as a "dependable yet slightly scruffy friend" resonate with your experiences in the industry? What challenges have you encountered that mirror this description?

2. Government Initiatives: What are your thoughts on the Infrastructure Investment and Jobs Act? How do you envision its impact on local communities and the construction industry as a whole?

3. Opportunities in Construction: In what ways do you think the current landscape presents a "buffet of opportunities" for contractors? What specific skills or strategies do you believe are essential to capitalize on these opportunities?

4. AI and Project Management: How do you see artificial intelligence transforming project management in construction? Can you think of a specific project where AI could have improved outcomes?

5. Risk Assessment with AI: Reflecting on the role of AI in risk assessment, how comfortable are you with the idea of relying on technology to evaluate potential risks in construction projects?

6. Technological Innovations: Which of the technologies mentioned (e.g., drones, 3D printing, IoT) do you believe will have the most significant impact on the future of construction? Why do you think that technology stands out?

7. Supplier Diversity: How does the idea of supplier diversity align with your understanding of sustainability in construction? What benefits do you think diverse suppliers bring to the industry?

8. Assessing Sustainability Practices: What methods do you think are most effective for assessing the sustainability practices of suppliers? How can these methods be improved?

9. Selecting Suppliers for Federal Contracts: In your experience, which factors do you believe are most critical when selecting construction companies for federal contracts? Why do you think these factors are prioritized?

10. Industry Organizations: How can joining industry organizations like AGC or ASCE benefit construction companies? Have you or your company participated in similar organizations, and

what was the experience like?

11. Continuous Improvement: Considering the quote, "Success is the sum of small efforts, repeated day in and day out," how do you apply this principle in your work? What small efforts have led to significant improvements in your projects?

12. Future of the Industry: As the construction industry evolves with new technologies and practices, what do you foresee as the biggest challenges and opportunities in the next five years?

13. Personal Reflection: How do you personally align with the commitment to sustainability and innovation in your work? What steps are you taking to contribute to a more resilient future in the construction industry?

These questions encourage deeper reflection on the themes presented in the text and promote critical thinking about the construction and infrastructure sector's evolving landscape.

## Conclusion

These sectors are not just cash cows; they're the whole barn! They play crucial roles in enhancing national security, improving public health, and modernizing our crumbling infrastructure. For aspiring entrepreneurs looking to dive into government contracting, focusing on one of these profitable sectors could be your golden ticket to success—like finding the last chocolate bar in a vending machine!

## Reflective Questions

- Which of these sectors aligns best with your business expertise and interests?

- What unique solutions can you bring to address the needs of agencies within these sectors?

- How can you leverage your existing network to explore opportunities in these profitable areas?

So, get ready to roll up your sleeves, dive into the paperwork, and maybe even grab a cape—because entering the government contracting world might just be the adventure you've been waiting for!

**Case Studies**

These case studies provide insights into the success of various companies within the four sectors of federal contracting:

**Case Studies for Defense and Security**

1. Lockheed Martin: [Lockheed Martin's Defense Contracting Success](https://www.lockheedmartin.com/en-us/news/press-releases/2021/2021-0224-lockheed-martin-secures-2020-spot-on-dod-top-100-contractors-list.html)

2. Northrop Grumman: [Northrop Grumman's Innovative Solutions](https://www.northropgrumman.com/what-we-do/defense/)

3. Raytheon Technologies: [Raytheon Technologies on

Cybersecurity and Defense](https://www.rtx.com/news/2021/raytheon-technologies-continues-to-support-us-defense-and-security)

## Case Studies for Information Technology (IT)

1. Boeing: [Boeing's IT Solutions for Defense and Commercial Sectors](https://www.boeing.com/features/innovation-quarterly/nov2019/feature-bds-digital-transformation.page)

2. IBM: [IBM's Partnerships with Government Agencies](https://www.ibm.com/industries/government)

3. Cisco Systems: [Cisco's Government Solutions and Contracts](https://www.cisco.com/c/en/us/solutions/government/overview.html)

## Case Studies for Healthcare

1. McKesson: [McKesson's Role in Government Contracts](https://www.mckesson.com/about-mckesson/mckesson-in-the-community/reports/mckesson-and-the-u-s-government/)

2. Cerner: [Cerner's Electronic Health Records Implementation](https://www.cerner.com/solutions/government)

3. Pfizer: [Pfizer's Vaccine Development and Government Collaboration](https://www.pfizer.com/news/press-release/press-release-detail/pfizer-announces-agreements-government-us-

vaccine)

## Case Studies for Construction and Infrastructure

1. Bechtel: [Bechtel's Infrastructure Projects](https://www.bechtel.com/projects/)

2. Kiewit: [Kiewit's Public Works Projects and Federal Contracts](https://www.kiewit.com/what-we-do/)

3. Fluor Corporation: [Fluor's Federal Contracting Success](https://www.fluor.com/projects/Pages/default.aspx)

# A Strategic Guide to Entering the Defense Sector of Government Contracting

Let's break down the process of entering the defense sector with a strategic, step-by-step guide that's as engaging as it is insightful.

And don't worry; we'll sprinkle in some Marvina snarkiness along the way!

## Step 1: Understand the Landscape

Checklist:

- Research the defense contracting environment: What's hot? What's not?

- Identify key players in the market, such as Lockheed Martin, Northrop Grumman, and Raytheon Technologies.

- Understand the major contracts currently being awarded and their value.

Marvina Insight: Think of this step as being a detective in a spy movie—gathering intel while trying not to trip over your own shoelaces.

# Step 2: Get Your DUNS Number

Process:

1. Visit the Dun & Bradstreet website.

2. Apply for a Data Universal Numbering System (DUNS) number. This unique nine-digit identifier is essential for doing business with the federal government.

3. Wait patiently (or not so patiently) for your DUNS number to be issued.

Regulation: The DUNS number is required for SAM registration, so don't skip this step unless you want to be left out in the cold!

Marvina Insight: Think of the DUNS number as your superhero cape—it gives you the power to fly into the world of federal contracting. Without it, you're just a regular Joe.

# Step 3: Register in the System for Award Management (SAM)

Process:

1. Go to the SAM website.

2. Create an account and fill out your business profile.

3. Provide information about your business type, size, and capabilities.

4. Submit your registration and wait for it to be processed.

Regulation: Ensure you comply with the Federal Acquisition Regulation (FAR) during this process.

**Checklist:**

- Have your DUNS number handy.

- Make sure to include your bank details for electronic payments (you want to get paid, right?).

Marvina Insight: Registering in SAM is like signing up for a new social media account—you'll have to provide all sorts of personal information and agree to terms you may not fully understand. Just remember to keep your password safe!

# Step 4: Familiarize Yourself with the FAR and DFARS

**Process:**

1. Access the Federal Acquisition Regulation (FAR) online.

2. Study the Defense Federal Acquisition Regulation Supplement (DFARS).

3. Take notes on sections relevant to your business and the contracts you're interested in.

Marvina Insight: Reading the FAR is like trying to decode an ancient language. Grab a cup of coffee (or two) and prepare for a brain workout. Just don't get too lost in the legal jargon—there's a plot twist around every corner!

# Step 5: Identify Your Niche

**Checklist:**

- Determine what products or services you can offer that meet the needs of the Department of Defense (DoD).

- Analyze the market for any gaps you could fill—think of yourself as a defense sector Robin Hood.

- Consider your existing capabilities and how they can be tailored to defense needs.

Marvina Insight: Finding your niche is like auditioning for a reality show—you've got to stand out from the crowd! So, what makes your offering the most interesting? Flashy dance moves? Unique product features? You decide!

# Step 6: Build Relationships and Network

**Process:**

1. Attend industry conferences, trade shows, and networking

events related to defense contracting.

2. Join associations like the National Defense Industrial Association (NDIA).

3. Connect with current contractors and defense agency representatives on LinkedIn.

Marvina Insight: Networking is like speed dating but for business. You'll want to make a lasting impression in just a few minutes, so bring your best elevator pitch—and maybe a fun fact or two to break the ice.

# Step 7: Develop a Winning Proposal

Process:

1. Monitor the Federal Business Opportunities (FBO) website for Requests for Proposals (RFPs).

2. Carefully read each RFP and note the requirements.

3. Create a proposal that clearly outlines how your business will meet or exceed the requirements.

4. Use persuasive language, data, and past performance examples to make your case.

5. Submit your proposal before the deadline (no pressure!).

Regulation: Ensure compliance with all outlined requirements in the RFP, as failing to do so could lead to disqualification.

Marvina Insight: Writing a proposal can feel like preparing for a final exam. You'll need to study the material, organize your thoughts, and maybe even pull an all-nighter to get it done. Just remember to breathe!

# Step 8: Understand Contract Types

## Checklist:

- Familiarize yourself with common contract types such as fixed-price, cost-plus, and time-and-materials contracts.

- Assess which type of contract aligns best with your offering and capabilities.

Marvina Insight: Understanding contract types is like knowing how to order at a diner—you need to know if you want the full meal or just a snack. Are you in it for the long haul or just dipping your toes in the water?

# Step 9: Stay Compliant with Regulations

Process:

1. Keep track of federal regulations and compliance requirements.

2. Regularly review your processes to ensure adherence to FAR and DFARS.

3. Stay updated on changes in regulations, as they can affect your contracts.

Marvina Insight: Compliance is like that annoying friend who always checks in—just when you think you're done, they remind you to stay on top of things. It's a continuous process, but it keeps you in the good graces of Uncle Sam!

# Step 10: Monitor Your Performance and Adapt

Checklist:

- Collect feedback from the government on your performance.

- Analyze your successes and areas for improvement.

- Adapt your strategies based on what you've learned to stay competitive.

Marvina Insight: Monitoring your performance is like watching a reality show about yourself. You get to see all the highs and lows and decide how to make the next season even better!

## Conclusion

Entering the defense contracting world may seem daunting. Still, with the right strategies, a dash of humor, and a willingness to navigate bureaucracy, you can carve out a niche in this lucrative sector. Remember, every superhero has to start somewhere—so put on your cape (or business suit) and get ready to make your mark!

# A Strategic Guide to Entering the IT Sector of Government Contracting

Welcome to the captivating world of IT contracting with the government! If you've ever dreamed of navigating a labyrinth of regulations while wielding your technical prowess like a lightsaber, you're in the right place. This detailed, step-by-step guide will help you enter the IT sector of government contracting with a mix of Marvina, insight, and a checklist to keep you on track. So, grab your favorite caffeinated beverage, and let's embark on this thrilling journey!

## Step 1: Understand the IT Landscape

Checklist:

- Research current trends in government IT needs: What software and services are agencies clamoring for?

- Identify key players in the market, such as IBM, Microsoft, and Cisco.

- Stay informed about agency budgets and spending priorities.

Marvina Insight: Think of this step as being a tech-savvy detective—you're on a mission to gather clues while avoiding the red tape that could trip you up like a rogue Wi-Fi signal.

# Step 2: Get Your DUNS Number

Process:

1. Visit the Dun & Bradstreet website.

2. Apply for a Data Universal Numbering System (DUNS) number. This unique nine-digit identifier is crucial for doing business with the federal government.

3. Wait for your DUNS number and do a little happy dance when it arrives.

Regulation: The DUNS number is necessary for registering in the System for Award Management (SAM), so don't skip this step unless you want to be left out in the cold!

Marvina Insight: Think of your DUNS number as your superhero identity—it's what transforms you from an ordinary civilian into a government contracting powerhouse!

# Step 3: Register in the System for Award Management (SAM)

Process:

1. Navigate to the SAM website.

2. Create an account and complete your business profile.

3. Provide essential information about your business type, size,

and capabilities.

4. Submit your registration and wait for confirmation. Patience is key here!

Regulation: Ensure you comply with the Federal Acquisition Regulation (FAR) during this process.

Checklist:

- Have your DUNS number ready.

- Include your bank details for electronic payments (because who doesn't love getting paid?).

Marvina Insight: Registering in SAM is like creating an online dating profile—you want to look good and catch the eye of potential partners. Just make sure to avoid any "catfishing"!

# Step 4: Familiarize Yourself with the FAR and DFARS

Process:

1. Access the Federal Acquisition Regulation (FAR) online.

2. Dive into the Defense Federal Acquisition Regulation Supplement (DFARS) to understand the specific rules governing defense contracts.

3. Take notes on sections relevant to IT contracting—your future self will thank you!

Marvina Insight: Reading the FAR is like trying to decipher a complex video game manual. Grab some snacks and settle in for a marathon of legal jargon—just don't forget to check for plot twists!

# Step 5: Identify Your Niche in IT

Checklist:

- Determine what IT products or services you can offer that align with government needs (think cybersecurity, software development, data management).

- Analyze the market for gaps you could fill—consider yourself a digital hero ready to save the day!

- Assess your existing capabilities and how they can be tailored to meet the unique demands of federal agencies.

Marvina Insight: Finding your niche is like auditioning for a talent show—you need to bring your A-game and showcase what makes you unique. Are you the tech version of a magician or a rock star?

# Step 6: Build Relationships and Network

Process:

1. Attend industry conferences, trade shows, and networking events focused on government IT contracting.

2. Join associations such as the Information Technology Industry

Council (ITI) or the National Defense Industrial Association (NDIA).

3. Connect with established contractors and agency representatives on LinkedIn—don't be shy!

Marvina Insight: Networking is like speed dating for businesses—make a memorable impression in a few minutes, and don't forget to prepare your best elevator pitch. A little charm goes a long way!

# Step 7: Monitor Federal Business Opportunities (FBO)

Process:

1. Regularly check the FBO website for Requests for Proposals (RFPs) relevant to your services.

2. Set up alerts to stay informed about new opportunities—you don't want to miss out on golden tickets!

3. Keep track of deadlines and requirements for each RFP.

Marvina Insight: Monitoring FBO is like being on a treasure hunt—each RFP is a hidden gem waiting to be discovered. Just make sure to pack your explorer's hat and a good sense of adventure!

# Step 8: Develop a Winning Proposal

Process:

1. Carefully read each RFP and understand the requirements.

2. Craft a proposal that clearly outlines how your IT solutions will meet or exceed those requirements.

3. Use data, case studies, and past performance examples to bolster your case.

4. Submit your proposal by the deadline (no pressure!).

Regulation: Ensure your proposal complies with all outlined requirements in the RFP—failing to do so could lead to disqualification.

Marvina Insight: Writing a proposal is like preparing for a big presentation—you want to impress your audience and leave them wanting more. Just remember to breathe and keep the typos at bay!

# Step 9: Understand Contract Types

Checklist:

- Familiarize yourself with common contract types in the IT sector, such as fixed-price, cost-plus, and time-and-materials contracts.

- Determine which type aligns best with your business model and offerings.

Marvina Insight: Understanding contract types is like knowing the difference between a latte and a cappuccino—each has its own flavor and purpose. Are you looking for something straightforward or a bit frothier?

# Step 10: Stay Compliant with Regulations

Process:

1. Track federal regulations and compliance requirements pertinent to IT contracting.

2. Regularly review your processes to ensure adherence to FAR and DFARS.

3. Stay updated on changes in regulations that might affect your contracts.

Marvina Insight: Compliance is like that diligent friend who always reminds you to return your library books on time—annoying but necessary for keeping your good standing!

# Step 11: Monitor Your Performance and Adapt

Checklist:

- Collect feedback from government clients on your performance.

- Analyze successes and identify areas for improvement.

- Adapt your strategies based on insights gathered to remain competitive.

Marvina Insight: Monitoring your performance is like watching your favorite reality show—keep track of the drama and plot twists, and decide how to write the next episode!

**Conclusion**

Entering the IT contracting world with the government can initially seem overwhelming, but with the right strategies, a sense of Marvina, and a willingness to tackle bureaucracy, you can successfully carve out your niche. Remember, every tech wizard has to start somewhere—so don your cape (or business attire) and prepare to make your mark in the IT sector of government contracting!

# A Strategic Guide to Entering the Healthcare Sector of Government Contracting

Welcome to the exhilarating world of healthcare contracting with the government! If you've ever wanted to navigate the complexities of regulations while using your expertise to make a difference, you've come to the right place. This detailed, step-by-step guide will help you enter the healthcare sector of government contracting with a mix of insight, Marvina, and a handy checklist to keep you on track. So, grab your stethoscope (or your favorite coffee mug), and let's get started!

# Step 1: Understand the Healthcare Landscape

Checklist:

- Research current trends in healthcare needs: What services and products are government agencies looking for?

- Identify key players in the market, such as McKesson, Cerner, and Siemens Healthineers.

- Stay informed about federal healthcare budgets and policies, especially those from agencies like the Department of Veterans Affairs (VA) and the Department of Health and Human Services (HHS).

Marvina Insight: Think of this step as being a healthcare detective—gathering clues while trying not to get lost in a maze of acronyms and regulations that could rival a medical textbook!

# Step 2: Get Your DUNS Number

Process:

1. Visit the Dun & Bradstreet website.

2. Apply for a Data Universal Numbering System (DUNS) number. This unique nine-digit identifier is crucial for doing business with the federal government.

3. Do a little happy dance when your DUNS number arrives.

Regulation: The DUNS number is necessary for registering in the System for Award Management (SAM), so don't skip this step unless you want to be left out in the cold!

Marvina Insight: Think of your DUNS number than your healthcare superhero ID—it's what transforms you from a regular business into a government contracting powerhouse!

# Step 3: Register in the System for Award Management (SAM)

Process:

1. Navigate to the SAM website.

2. Create an account and complete your business profile.

3. Provide essential information about your business type, size, and capabilities.

4. Submit your registration and wait for confirmation. Patience is key here!

Regulation: Ensure you comply with the Federal Acquisition Regulation (FAR) during this process.

Checklist:

- Have your DUNS number ready.

- Include your bank details for electronic payments (because who doesn't love getting paid?).

Marvina Insight: Registering in SAM is like filling out a medical history form—it can feel tedious, but it's essential for getting the care (or contracts) you need!

# Step 4: Familiarize Yourself with the FAR and HHS Regulations

Process:

1. Access the Federal Acquisition Regulation (FAR) online.

2. Dive into specific healthcare regulations issued by the HHS, including those governing procurement in the healthcare sector.

3. Take notes on sections relevant to healthcare contracting— your future self will thank you!

Marvina Insight: Reading the FAR and HHS regulations is like studying for a big exam. Grab some snacks, buckle up, and prepare to dive into the world of legal jargon—just don't forget to check for plot twists!

# Step 5: Identify Your Niche in Healthcare

Checklist:

- Determine what healthcare products or services you can offer that align with government needs (think medical supplies, telehealth services, or health IT solutions).

- Analyze the market for gaps you could fill—consider yourself a healthcare hero ready to save the day!

- Assess your existing capabilities and how they can be tailored to meet the unique demands of federal agencies.

Marvina Insight: Finding your niche is like auditioning for a reality show—you need to bring your A-game and showcase what makes you unique. Are you the healthcare version of a magician or a rock star?

# Step 6: Build Relationships and Network

Process:

1. Attend industry conferences, trade shows, and networking events focused on healthcare contracting.

2. Join associations such as the Healthcare Information and Management Systems Society (HIMSS) or the National Association of Government Contractors (NAGC).

3. Connect with established contractors and agency representatives on LinkedIn—don't be shy!

Marvina Insight: Networking is like speed dating for businesses—make a memorable impression in a few minutes, and don't forget to prepare your best elevator pitch. A little charm goes a long way!

# Step 7: Monitor Federal Business Opportunities (FBO)

Process:

1. Regularly check the FBO website for Requests for Proposals (RFPs) relevant to your services.

2. Set up alerts to stay informed about new opportunities—you don't want to miss out on golden tickets!

3. Keep track of deadlines and requirements for each RFP.

Marvina Insight: Monitoring FBO is like being on a treasure hunt—each RFP is a hidden gem waiting to be discovered. Just make sure to pack your explorer's hat and a good sense of adventure!

# Step 8: Develop a Winning Proposal

Process:

1. Carefully read each RFP and understand the requirements.

2. Craft a proposal that clearly outlines how your healthcare solutions will meet or exceed those requirements.

3. Use data, case studies, and past performance examples to bolster your case.

4. Submit your proposal by the deadline (no pressure!).

Regulation: Ensure your proposal complies with all outlined requirements in the RFP—failing to do so could lead to disqualification.

Marvina Insight: Writing a proposal is like preparing for a big presentation—you want to impress your audience and leave them wanting more. Just remember to breathe and keep the typos at bay!

# Step 9: Understand Contract Types

Checklist:

- Familiarize yourself with common contract types in the healthcare sector, such as fixed-price, cost-plus, and time-and-materials contracts.

- Determine which type aligns best with your business model and offerings.

Marvina Insight: Understanding contract types is like knowing the difference between over-the-counter and prescription medications—each has its own use and implications. Are you looking for something straightforward or a bit more complex?

# Step 10: Stay Compliant with Regulations

Process:

1. Track federal regulations and compliance requirements pertinent to healthcare contracting.

2. Regularly review your processes to ensure adherence to FAR and HHS regulations.

3. Stay updated on changes in regulations that might affect your contracts.

Marvina Insight: Compliance is like that diligent friend who always reminds you to take your vitamins—annoying, but necessary for maintaining your good standing!

# Step 11: Monitor Your Performance and Adapt

Checklist:

- Collect feedback from government clients on your performance.

- Analyze successes and identify areas for improvement.

- Adapt your strategies based on insights gathered to remain competitive.

Marvina Insight: Monitoring your performance is like watching your favorite medical drama—keep track of the twists and turns and decide how to write the next episode!

**Conclusion**

Entering the healthcare contracting world with the government can initially seem overwhelming, but with the right strategies, a sense of Marvina, and a willingness to tackle bureaucracy, you can successfully carve out your niche. Remember, every healthcare hero has to start somewhere—so don your cape (or business attire) and prepare to make your mark in the healthcare sector of government contracting!

# A Strategic Guide to Entering the Construction and Infrastructure Sector of Government Contracting

Welcome to the dynamic world of construction and infrastructure contracting with the government! If you've ever dreamed of building bridges (literally and figuratively) while navigating a maze of regulations, you're in the right place. This detailed, step-by-step guide will help you enter the construction and infrastructure sector of government contracting with a mix of insight, Marvina, and handy checklists to keep you on track. So, grab your hard hat (or favorite coffee mug), and let's get started!

# Step 1: Understand the Construction Landscape

Checklist:

- Research current trends in government infrastructure needs: What projects are on the horizon?

- Identify key players in the market, such as Bechtel, Kiewit, and Fluor Corporation.

- Stay informed about federal budgets and policies, especially those related to transportation, housing, and public works.

Marvina Insight: Think of this step as being a construction detective—gathering clues while trying not to get buried under a mountain of paperwork and red tape!

# Step 2: Get Your DUNS Number

Process:

1. Visit the Dun & Bradstreet website.

2. Apply for a Data Universal Numbering System (DUNS) number. This unique nine-digit identifier is crucial for doing business with the federal government.

3. Do a little happy dance when your DUNS number arrives.

Regulation: The DUNS number is necessary for registering in the System for Award Management (SAM), so don't skip this step unless you want to be left out in the cold!

Marvina Insight: Think of your DUNS number as your construction superhero ID—it's what transforms you from a regular business into a government contracting powerhouse!

# Step 3: Register in the System for Award Management (SAM)

Process:

1. Navigate to the SAM website.

2. Create an account and complete your business profile.

3. Provide essential information about your business type, size, and capabilities.

4. Submit your registration and wait for confirmation. Patience is key here!

Regulation: Ensure you comply with the Federal Acquisition Regulation (FAR) during this process.

Checklist:

- Have your DUNS number ready.

- Include your bank details for electronic payments (because who doesn't love getting paid?).

Marvina Insight: Registering in SAM is like filling out a job application—it can feel tedious, but it's essential for getting the gig (or contracts) you need!

# Step 4: Familiarize Yourself with the FAR and Construction Regulations

Process:

1. Access the Federal Acquisition Regulation (FAR) online.

2. Dive into specific construction regulations issued by agencies like the Department of Transportation (DOT) and the Army Corps of Engineers.

3. Take notes on sections relevant to construction contracting—your future self will thank you!

Marvina Insight: Reading the FAR and construction regulations is like studying for a big exam. Grab some snacks, buckle up, and prepare to dive into the world of legal jargon—just don't forget to check for plot twists!

# Step 5: Identify Your Niche in Construction

Checklist:

- Determine what construction services you can offer that align with government needs (think road construction, public buildings, or infrastructure repair).

- Analyze the market for gaps you could fill—consider yourself a construction hero ready to save the day!

- Assess your existing capabilities and how they can be tailored to meet the unique demands of federal agencies.

Marvina Insight: Finding your niche is like auditioning for a talent show—you need to bring your A-game and showcase what makes you unique. Are you the construction version of a magician or a rock star?

# Step 6: Build Relationships and Network

Process:

1. Attend industry conferences, trade shows, and networking events focused on construction and infrastructure contracting.

2. Join associations such as the National Association of Government Contractors (NAGC) or the Associated General Contractors of America (AGC).

3. Connect with established contractors and agency representatives on LinkedIn—don't be shy!

Marvina Insight: Networking is like speed dating for businesses—make a memorable impression in a few minutes, and don't forget to prepare your best elevator pitch. A little charm goes a long way!

# Step 7: Monitor Federal Business Opportunities (FBO)

Process:

1. Regularly check the FBO website for Requests for Proposals (RFPs) relevant to your services.

2. Set up alerts to stay informed about new opportunities—you don't want to miss out on golden tickets!

3. Keep track of deadlines and requirements for each RFP.

Marvina Insight: Monitoring FBO is like being on a treasure hunt—each RFP is a hidden gem waiting to be discovered. Just make sure to pack your explorer's hat and a good sense of adventure!

# Step 8: Develop a Winning Proposal

Process:

1. Carefully read each RFP and understand the requirements.

2. Craft a proposal that clearly outlines how your construction services will meet or exceed those requirements.

3. Use data, case studies, and past performance examples to bolster your case.

4. Submit your proposal by the deadline (no pressure!).

Regulation: Ensure your proposal complies with all outlined requirements in the RFP—failing to do so could lead to disqualification.

Marvina Insight: Writing a proposal is like preparing for a big presentation—you want to impress your audience and leave them wanting more. Just remember to breathe and keep the typos at bay!

# Step 9: Understand Contract Types

Checklist:

- Familiarize yourself with common contract types in the construction sector, such as fixed-price, cost-plus, and time-and-materials contracts.

- Determine which type aligns best with your business model and offerings.

Marvina Insight: Understanding contract types is like knowing the difference between a hammer and a drill—each has its own use and implications. Are you looking for something straightforward or a bit more complex?

# Step 10: Stay Compliant with Regulations

Process:

1. Track federal regulations and compliance requirements pertinent to construction contracting.

2. Regularly review your processes to ensure adherence to FAR and agency-specific regulations.

3. Stay updated on changes in regulations that might affect your contracts.

Marvina Insight: Compliance is like that diligent friend who always reminds you to wear a hard hat on the job site—annoying but necessary for keeping you safe and sound!

# Step 11: Monitor Your Performance and Adapt

Checklist:

- Collect feedback from government clients on your performance.

- Analyze successes and identify areas for improvement.

- Adapt your strategies based on insights gathered to remain competitive.

Marvina Insight: Monitoring your performance is like watching a construction reality show—keep track of the drama and plot twists, and decide how to write the next episode!

Conclusion

Entering the construction and infrastructure contracting world with the government can initially seem overwhelming, but with the right strategies, a sense of Marvina, and a willingness to tackle bureaucracy, you can successfully carve out your niche. Remember, every construction hero has to start somewhere—so don your hard hat (or business attire) and prepare to make your mark in the construction sector of government contracting!

# The Ultimate Resource

Apex Accelerator is a program designed to support small businesses, particularly those looking to expand their market presence or engage in government contracting. The program is free, making it accessible to a wide range of entrepreneurs and startups. Here are some key reasons why Apex Accelerator is beneficial:

1. Expert Guidance: Businesses receive expert advice on navigating the complexities of government contracting, including proposal writing and compliance.

2. Workshops and Training: The program offers various workshops that cover essential topics such as marketing strategies, financial management, and business development.

3. Networking Opportunities: Participants can connect with other small businesses and potential partners, fostering collaborations that can lead to new opportunities.

4. Resource Access: Apex Accelerator provides access to valuable resources, including market research tools and databases, to help businesses identify opportunities.

5. Customized Support: Each business receives tailored assistance based on its unique needs and goals, ensuring that the

support provided is effective and relevant.

# How to Access Apex Accelerator

1. Visit the Website: Interested businesses can begin by visiting the official Apex Accelerator website, which provides detailed information about the program and its offerings.

2. Find Your States Program: Since Apex Accelerator operates in various states, it's important to locate the specific program available in your state. Each state may have a local office or partner organization that administers the program.

3. Sign Up: Businesses can register for the program through the state-specific website. This often involves filling out a registration form and providing basic information about the business.

4. Participate in Activities: Once registered, businesses can start participating in workshops, training sessions, and networking events offered by the program.

# State-Specific Websites

To find the Apex Accelerator program in each state, you can visit the following links:

1. Alabama: https://www.alabamaapexaccelerator.com

2. Alaska: https://www.alaskaapexaccelerator.com

3. Arizona: https://www.arizonaapexaccelerator.com

4. Arkansas: https://www.arkansasapexaccelerator.com

5. California: https://www.californiaapexaccelerator.com

6. Colorado: https://www.coloradoapexaccelerator.com

7. Connecticut: https://www.connecticutapexaccelerator.com

8. Delaware: https://www.delawareapexaccelerator.com

9. Florida: https://www.floridaapexaccelerator.com

10. Georgia: https://www.georgiaapexaccelerator.com

11. Hawaii: https://www.hawaiiapexaccelerator.com

12. Idaho: https://www.idahoapexaccelerator.com

13. Illinois: https://www.illinoisapexaccelerator.com

14. Indiana: https://www.indianaapexaccelerator.com

15. Iowa: https://www.iowaapexaccelerator.com

16. Kansas: https://www.kansasapexaccelerator.com

17. Kentucky: https://www.kentuckyapexaccelerator.com

18. Louisiana: https://www.louisianaapexaccelerator.com

19. Maine: https://www.maineapexaccelerator.com

20. Maryland: https://www.marylandapexaccelerator.com

21.Massachusetts: https://www.massachusettsapexaccelerator.com

22. Michigan: https://www.michiganapexaccelerator.com

23. Minnesota: https://www.minnesotaapexaccelerator.com

24. Mississippi: https://www.mississippiapexaccelerator.com

25. Missouri: https://www.missouriapexaccelerator.com

26. Montana: https://www.montanaapexaccelerator.com

27. Nebraska: https://www.nebraskaapexaccelerator.com

28. Nevada: https://www.nevadaapexaccelerator.com

29. New Hampshire:
https://www.newhampshireapexaccelerator.com

30. New Jersey: https://www.newjerseyapexaccelerator.com

31. New Mexico: https://www.newmexicoapexaccelerator.com

32. New York: https://www.newyorkapexaccelerator.com

33. North Carolina:
https://www.northcarolinaapexaccelerator.com

34. North Dakota: https://www.northdakotaapexaccelerator.com

35. Ohio: https://www.ohioapexaccelerator.com

36. Oklahoma: https://www.oklahomaapexaccelerator.com

37. Oregon: https://www.oregonapexaccelerator.com

38. Pennsylvania:
https://www.pennsylvaniaapexaccelerator.com

39. Rhode Island: https://www.rhodeislandapexaccelerator.com

40. South Carolina:
https://www.southcarolinaapexaccelerator.com

41. South Dakota: https://www.southdakotaapexaccelerator.com

42. Tennessee: https://www.tennesseeapexaccelerator.com

43. Texas: https://www.texasapexaccelerator.com

44. Utah: https://www.utahapexaccelerator.com

45. Vermont: https://www.vermontapexaccelerator.com

46. Virginia: https://www.virginiaapexaccelerator.com

47. Washington: https://www.washingtonapexaccelerator.com

48. West Virginia:
https://www.westvirginiaapexaccelerator.com

49. Wisconsin: https://www.wisconsinapexaccelerator.com

50. Wyoming: https://www.wyomingapexaccelerator.com

These links will direct you to the specific resources and contacts for each state's Apex Accelerator program, providing you with the support needed to grow your business successfully.

# The Beginner's Guide to Networking: How to Make Connections Without Losing Your Mind (or Your Dignity)

Welcome to the world of networking! Whether you're trying to climb the corporate ladder, find a mentor, or just meet interesting people, networking is a vital skill. But fear not! This guide will help you navigate the sometimes awkward, often Marvina world of networking with step-by-step actions that will have you connecting like a pro in no time. So, grab your business cards, put on your best smile, and let's dive in!

# Step 1: Prepare Yourself (and Your Elevator Pitch)

Action:

- Craft Your Elevator Pitch: This is your chance to introduce yourself in about 30 seconds. Think of it as a mini-commercial for YOU. Include your name, what you do, and a fun fact that makes you memorable. For example: "Hi, I'm Jane, a software developer who specializes in creating apps that help users find the nearest coffee shop. Fun fact: I can drink a whole pot of coffee in one sitting!"

Marvina Tip: Practice in front of a mirror or your pet. They may not give you feedback, but at least they'll listen without interrupting!

# Step 2: Choose Your Networking Events Wisely

Action:

- Find Events: Look for industry conferences, local meetups, or webinars where you can meet people in your field. Websites like

Meetup, Eventbrite, or even LinkedIn can help you find opportunities.

Marvina Tip: Avoid events that sound like they could be held in a creepy basement unless you're into that sort of thing. "Networking with ghosts" probably won't look good on your resume.

# Step 3: Dress to Impress (but Stay Comfortable)

Action:

- Pick Your Outfit: Choose professional attire that makes you feel confident and comfortable. Remember, you might be standing for a while, so wear shoes that won't make you feel like you're walking on hot coals.

Marvina Tip: Avoid wearing anything too flashy unless you want to be that person everyone remembers for their neon green tie or sequined blazer. "Hey, remember that guy who looked like he just walked out of a disco? Yeah, I don't think he got any business cards out."

# Step 4: Arrive Early (or Fashionably Late)

Action:

- Get There Early: Arriving early gives you a chance to settle in and chat with the first few people who arrive. It's less intimidating than walking into a room full of strangers.

Marvina Tip: If you arrive late, just pretend you were making a grand entrance. "Oh, sorry, I got stuck in traffic. You know how it is with all the... um... traffic!"

# Step 5: Start Conversations (and Keep Them Going)

Action:

- Approach Someone: Smile, introduce yourself, and use your elevator pitch. Ask open-ended questions to keep the conversation flowing, such as "What brought you to this event?" or "What's your favorite part of working in this industry?"

Marvina Tip: If the conversation stalls, just throw in a random fact like, "Did you know octopuses have three hearts?" It might confuse them, but at least it's memorable!

# Step 6: Use Your Listening Skills (Yes, You Can Do It!)

Action:

- Listen Actively: Show genuine interest in what the other person is saying. Nodding, maintaining eye contact, and asking follow-up questions will make you a great conversationalist.

Marvina Tip: Try not to zone out and start thinking about what's for dinner. "I'm sorry, what were you saying? I got distracted thinking about tacos."

# Step 7: Collect Business Cards (or Create Your Own)

Action:

- Exchange Information: When the conversation is wrapping up, ask for their business card and offer yours in return. If you don't have a card, don't sweat it; you can always connect on LinkedIn.

Marvina Tip: If you don't have a business card, just scribble your details on a napkin. "This is my official 'napkin card'—very exclusive!"

# Step 8: Follow-Up (But Don't Stalk)

Action:

- Send a Follow-Up Email: Within 24-48 hours, send a personalized email thanking them for the conversation. Mention something specific you talked about reminding them who you are.

Marvina Tip: Avoid sending messages every day. You're trying to build a connection, not become their new best friend who texts at 3 AM. "Hey, just checking if you've thought about my taco fact yet!"

# Step 9: Attend More Events (Rinse and Repeat)

Action:

- Keep Networking: The more you practice, the better you'll get. Attend more events, meet new people, and refine your pitch. Networking is a marathon, not a sprint!

Marvina Tip: Consider bringing a friend or colleague for moral support. It's like having a wingman for networking. "I'll distract them, and you can swoop in for the business card!"

# Step 10: Reflect and Improve

Action:

- Evaluate Your Experience: After each event, take a moment to reflect on what went well and what could be improved. Adjust your approach accordingly for next time.

Marvina Tip: If you bombed an interaction, just chalk it up to "networking experience." "Well, I may have accidentally asked if they were robots, but at least I learned not to do that again!"

Conclusion

Networking doesn't have to be a daunting task filled with anxiety and awkwardness. With a little preparation, a sprinkle of Marvina, and a willingness to engage, you'll find yourself building valuable connections in no time. Remember, everyone else is just as nervous as you are, so go out there, make those connections, and most importantly, have fun doing it!

# Acronym Overload: A Snarky Guide to Federal Contracting Lingo

Here's a detailed list of common acronyms and their meanings in the context of federal contracting in the United States. Because let's face it, if you're diving into this bureaucratic jungle, you're going to need a decoder ring to make sense of all these letters!

Acronyms in Federal Contracting

1. AFB - Air Force Base

2. AFA - Air Force Association

3. AFRL - Air Force Research Laboratory

4. AIA - Aerospace Industries Association

5. BPA - Blanket Purchase Agreement

6. CA - Contracting Officer's Representative (COR) Agreement

7. CBA - Collective Bargaining Agreement

8. CCF - Contract Change Form

9. CFDA - Catalog of Federal Domestic Assistance

10. CFR - Code of Federal Regulations

11. COTS - Commercial Off-The-Shelf

12. DCAA - Defense Contract Audit Agency

13. DCMA - Defense Contract Management Agency

14. DOD - Department of Defense

15. DOE - Department of Energy

16. DOI - Department of the Interior

17. DOL - Department of Labor

18. EDWOSB - Economically Disadvantaged Women-Owned Small Business

19. FAR - Federal Acquisition Regulation

20. FBO - Federal Business Opportunities (now beta.SAM.gov)

21. FCA - Federal Contracting Authority

22. FCS - Federal Contracting System

23. GSA - General Services Administration

24. HHS - Department of Health and Human Services

25. IDIQ - Indefinite Delivery/Indefinite Quantity

26. IT - Information Technology

27. LPTA - Lowest Price Technically Acceptable

28. M&O - Management and Operations

29. NAICS - North American Industry Classification System

30. NDA - Non-Disclosure Agreement

31. NIST - National Institute of Standards and Technology

32. OASIS - One Acquisition Solution for Integrated Services

33. OIG - Office of Inspector General

34. PBA - Performance-Based Acquisition

35. POC - Point of Contact

36. PR - Purchase Request

37. PSR - Performance System Review

38. RFP - Request for Proposal

39. RFQ - Request for Quotation

40. RFI - Request for Information

41. SAM - System for Award Management

42. SBA - Small Business Administration

43. SDVOSB - Service-Disabled Veteran-Owned Small Business

44. SOW - Statement of Work

45. SOO - Statement of Objectives

46. T&M - Time and Materials

47. TAA - Trade Agreements Act

48. WOSB - Women-Owned Small Business


Additional Acronyms Related to Federal Contracting

1. CPFF - Cost-Plus-Fixed-Fee

2. CPPC - Cost-Plus-Percentage of Cost

3. FMS - Foreign Military Sales

4. IDIQ - Indefinite Delivery/Indefinite Quantity

5. LPTA - Lowest Price Technically Acceptable

6. PWS - Performance Work Statement

7. SBA - Small Business Administration

8. VOSB - Veteran-Owned Small Business

This list covers a range of acronyms commonly used in federal contracting. Understanding these terms is crucial for navigating the complexities of government contracting and can help streamline communication and comprehension within the industry. Now go forth and conquer that acronym soup!

# Swiss Army Knife Glossary

Here's a glossary of common federal government terms that are as useful as a Swiss Army knife for navigating the complexities of federal contracting and government operations. Grab your coffee and get ready to decode the bureaucratic mumbo jumbo!

Federal Government Terms Glossary

1. Acquisition: The process of obtaining goods or services, including the planning, awarding, and management of contracts. Think of it as the government's shopping spree but with way more paperwork.

2. Bid: A formal offer submitted by a contractor in response to a Request for Proposal (RFP) or Request for Quotation (RFQ). It's like trying to impress someone on a date with your best offer.

3. Contract: A legally binding agreement between two or more parties that outlines the terms and conditions for providing goods or services. Basically, it's the fine print that keeps everyone in line.

4. Contracting Officer (CO): A government employee authorized to enter into, administer, and terminate contracts on behalf of the federal government. They're like the referees in the game of government contracting—without them, chaos ensues.

5. DUNS Number: Data Universal Numbering System number, a unique nine-digit identifier assigned to businesses for government contracting purposes. It's like your business's social security number but for federal contracts.

6. Federal Acquisition Regulation (FAR): The primary set of rules governing federal government procurement processes. Think of it as the rulebook for everyone trying to get a piece of Uncle Sam's pie.

7. Indefinite Delivery/Indefinite Quantity (IDIQ): A type of contract that provides for an indefinite quantity of supplies or services during a fixed period, allowing flexibility in ordering. It's the "we'll take as many as we need" approach to contracts.

8. Request for Proposal (RFP): A document issued by a

government agency inviting contractors to submit proposals for a specific project or service. It's the government's way of saying, "Show us what you've got!"

9. Request for Quotation (RFQ): A document used to solicit price quotes from suppliers for specific products or services. Basically, it's the government asking for the best deal—like shopping for shoes but with less fun.

10. Small Business Administration (SBA): A government agency that provides support to small businesses, including assistance with federal contracting. Think of them as the cheerleaders for small businesses trying to get in the game.

11. System for Award Management (SAM): A federal government system that consolidates the capabilities of multiple procurement systems, allowing businesses to register and apply for government contracts. It's like the online portal where all the magic happens.

12. Sole Source Contract: A contract awarded without a competitive bidding process, typically because only one supplier can provide the required goods or services. It's the government's way of saying, "You're the only one for us."

13. Cost-Plus Contract: A type of contract where the contractor is reimbursed for allowable costs incurred plus an additional amount for profit. It's like saying, "We'll cover your expenses plus give you a little extra for your trouble."

14. Fixed-Price Contract: A contract that establishes a set price for the goods or services provided, regardless of the actual costs incurred. It's a straightforward deal—what you see is what you get.

15. Performance Work Statement (PWS): A document that

outlines the specific tasks and outcomes expected from a contractor in a performance-based contract. It's like a detailed job description, but for contracts.

16. Statement of Work (SOW): A detailed description of the work required for a specific project, including the objectives, deliverables, and timeline. It's your roadmap for getting the job done.

17. Federal Business Opportunities (FBO): A website that provides information on federal procurement opportunities, including RFPs and contract awards. It's where all the action is for contractors looking to snag a government deal.

18. GSA Schedule: A long-term governmentwide contract with commercial firms providing access to millions of commercial products and services at volume discount pricing. It's the government's version of a bulk shopping club.

19. Subcontractor: A business that enters into a contract with a prime contractor to provide specific services or products for a government project. They're the behind-the-scenes heroes making sure everything runs smoothly.

20. Set-Aside: A government contracting program that reserves a certain percentage of contracts for specific categories of businesses, such as small businesses, women-owned businesses, or veteran-owned businesses. It's like giving certain companies a VIP pass to the contracting party.

21. Source Selection: The process of evaluating proposals and selecting a contractor based on established criteria outlined in the RFP. It's the "who gets the rose" moment in the contracting world.

22. Bureaucracy: A system of government characterized by strict rules and regulations, often leading to complex processes and red tape. It's the reason why some contracts take longer to get approved than it takes to binge-watch a whole series.

23. Compliance: Adhering to laws, regulations, and guidelines applicable to federal contracting and procurement processes. It's the part of the job that keeps you on the straight and narrow.

24. Market Research: The process of gathering information about the market, including potential suppliers, pricing, and industry trends, to inform procurement decisions. It's like doing your homework before asking someone out.

25. Negotiation: The process of discussing contract terms and conditions between the government and the contractor to reach a mutual agreement. It's where the magic (and sometimes drama) happens in securing the deal.

This glossary provides an overview of essential terms used in federal contracting and government operations, helping individuals better understand the language of the industry. Now go forth and conquer that acronym soup because we all know the government loves its letters!

# Help a Federal Employee Out

Ah, federal employees and their epic quest for contracting glory! It's like trying to navigate a maze designed by M.C. Escher while wearing a blindfold and juggling flaming torches. But fear not, dear contractors! Your expertise is here to save the day, much like Batman swooping in to rescue Gotham from bureaucratic chaos.

Let's break down the challenges these brave souls face and how you can swoop in with your superhero capes (or business suits) to save the day.

1. **Complex Regulations**:

   - **Challenge**: Welcome to the labyrinth of regulations, also known as FAR (Federal Acquisition Regulation), where compliance is as elusive as Bigfoot.

   - **How Contractors Can Help**: Think of yourselves as the wise Gandalf guiding the federal Frodo through the treacherous terrain of red tape. With your navigational expertise, you can help them avoid compliance-induced migraines and ensure they don't accidentally sign away their firstborn.

2. **Bureaucratic Delays**:

   - **Challenge**: The contracting process moves slower than a sloth on a lazy Sunday. Seriously, it's like watching paint dry—if the paint were made of molasses.

   - **How Contractors Can Help**: Put on your best superhero cape and present streamlined proposals that make approvals happen faster than the Millennium Falcon making the Kessel Run. You'll be the unsung heroes speeding up the process while everyone else is still stuck in traffic.

3. **Limited Resources**:

   - **Challenge**: Federal employees are often juggling more contracts than a circus performer, and let's be honest—no one wants to end up as the clown.

- **How Contractors Can Help**: Take the reins on project management. Think of yourselves as the trusty sidekick who takes care of the logistics while the federal employee can focus on their superhero duties. Regular updates mean they'll never have to ask, "What's going on?" again.

4. **Lack of Technical Expertise**:

- **Challenge**: Sometimes, federal employees are about as tech-savvy as your grandma trying to figure out TikTok.

- **How Contractors Can Help**: Step in with your specialized skills and knowledge. You're the Yoda they didn't know they needed—offering training and support while ensuring projects meet those technical standards. "Do or do not, there is no try," but with you, they're more likely to "do."

5. **Inadequate Communication**:

- **Challenge**: Poor communication can turn into a game of telephone, resulting in misunderstandings that would make even the most patient person lose their cool.

- **How Contractors Can Help**: Establish clear lines of communication like a well-timed sitcom punchline. Use project management tools to keep everyone aligned so they're not left wondering if they're on the same page or just reading different books entirely.

6. **Performance Monitoring**:

- **Challenge**: Monitoring contractor performance can feel like herding cats—frustrating and often futile.

- **How Contractors Can Help**: Set clear performance metrics and KPIs from day one. You'll provide the transparency needed to keep the performance reviews smooth, much like a well-choreographed dance number on Broadway.

7. **Budget Constraints**:

- **Challenge**: Federal agencies are often tighter with their budgets than Scrooge McDuck in a penny-pinching contest.

- **How Contractors Can Help**: Offer flexible pricing models and innovative solutions that won't break the bank. You can be the financial fairy godparent, waving your wand to identify cost-saving opportunities that make dreams come true without sacrificing quality.

8. **Changing Requirements**:

- **Challenge**: Federal projects often shift priorities faster than a contestant on *The Bachelor* trying to win a rose.

- **How Contractors Can Help**: Build flexibility into your proposals. You're the seasoned negotiator who can facilitate discussions on scope changes without causing any drama—think of yourself as the ultimate mediator in a reality TV showdown.

9. **Risk Management**:

- **Challenge**: Conducting thorough risk assessments might feel like trying to find Waldo in a crowd—overwhelming and slightly impossible.

- **How Contractors Can Help**: Perform risk assessments and develop mitigation strategies. You'll help federal employees spot potential issues early, giving them the foresight of a Marvel superhero predicting the next big crisis.

10. **Training and Development**:

- **Challenge**: Federal employees need ongoing training to keep up with best practices, but who has the time with all the chaos?

- **How Contractors Can Help**: Offer training sessions or workshops that equip them with the knowledge and skills they need. You'll be their Obi-Wan, guiding them through the galaxy of contracting and procurement.

By understanding these challenges and swooping in with tailored solutions, contractors can be the heroes federal employees didn't know they needed. Together, you can conquer the contracting process and turn "bureaucratic bliss" into a smooth and successful endeavor. As the great Yoda once said, "Do or do not, there is no try." So, let's do this!

# Navigating the Insurance Jungle: A Snarky Guide for Government Contractors

So, you've decided to dip your toes into the thrilling world of federal contracting? Congratulations! But before you dive in headfirst like a kid off the high dive, let's chat about something almost as important as your business plan: insurance. Yes, that's right—insurance. The necessary evil that keeps your business afloat when the unexpected crashes the party like an uninvited relative at Thanksgiving dinner.

Steps to Obtain Insurance: Your Roadmap to Coverage

1. Assess Your Needs:

Before you can hustle for quotes, figure out what kind of insurance you actually need. General liability? Check. Professional liability? You betcha. Workers' compensation? Absolutely—unless you enjoy throwing money at lawsuits. Depending on your niche (construction, IT, healthcare), tailor your coverage. Remember, it's like shopping for a suit; you wouldn't wear a tuxedo to a barbecue.

2. Research Insurance Providers:

Not all insurance companies are created equal. Look for those that specialize in contractor coverage and have experience with government contracts. Think of it as finding a doctor who knows what they're doing—would you trust a dentist to perform heart surgery? I didn't think so.

3. Gather Necessary Documentation:

Time to channel your inner accountant. Prepare your DUNS number, business registration details, and any previous contracts you've worked on. It's like packing for a trip—if you forget your passport, you're not going anywhere.

4. Get Quotes:

Contact multiple insurance providers for quotes. This is your chance to shop around like you're at a flea market, but remember to provide the same information to each provider for an apples-to-apples comparison. Don't be that person who shows up at a potluck with a store-bought pie when everyone else made theirs from scratch!

5. Review Policies:

This is where the fun really begins—sifting through terms, coverage limits, and exclusions. Make sure what you're signing up for actually covers what you need. It's like reading the fine print before you sign up for that "free" trial that suddenly turns into a monthly subscription.

6. Consult with an Insurance Agent:

Feeling overwhelmed? Call in the experts. An insurance agent who specializes in government contracting can help navigate the complexities of the insurance world. Think of them as your personal guide through a bureaucratic jungle.

7. Purchase the Policy:

Once you've found the right provider and policy, it's time to seal the deal. Be prepared to fork over that initial premium payment—because nothing in life is free, my friend.

8. Maintain Compliance:

Keep your insurance coverage updated and in line with any additional requirements from your government contracts. Think of it as keeping your car maintained; neglecting it will only lead to more significant problems down the road.

Why Insurance Matters for Government Contractors?

Now, you might be thinking, "Why do I need insurance? Isn't it just another expense?" Well, let me hit you with some reality:

1. Compliance Requirements:

Many federal contracts demand specific insurance. If you don't have them, you might as well be trying to win a game of Monopoly without any money—good luck with that!

2. Liability Protection:

Accidents happen. Whether it's a slip and fall on a job site or a disgruntled client who didn't like your work, insurance helps protect you from the legal fallout. Just ask any contractor who's had to deal with a lawsuit after a mishap.

3. Financial Security:

Insurance acts like a financial safety net. If something goes wrong—like the time a construction crew accidentally took out a power line—insurance can save your business from going belly up.

4. Credibility and Trust:

Having the right insurance demonstrates to clients that you're a professional who takes risks seriously. It's like showing up to a job interview in a suit instead of pajamas.

5. Risk Management:

Insurance is a key player in your risk management strategy. It helps you anticipate potential challenges and prepare for them. As the saying goes, "Hope for the best but prepare for the worst."

Must-Have Insurances for Government Contractors

So, what's on your insurance shopping list? Here are the

essentials:

1. General Liability Insurance:

The bread and butter of contractor insurance, covering bodily injury and property damage.

2. Professional Liability Insurance:

This one's for when things go sideways due to negligence or mistakes. Think of it as your "oops" coverage.

3. Workers' Compensation Insurance:

Mandatory in most states—this protects your employees and your wallet if someone gets hurt on the job.

4. Commercial Auto Insurance:

If you're using vehicles for business, this is a must. You don't want to be caught driving a work vehicle without it after hitting a pothole.

5. Product Liability Insurance:

For manufacturers or distributors, this covers claims related to product defects. Just ask any toy company that's had to deal with a recall.

6. Cyber Liability Insurance:

Important for IT contractors, this protects against data breaches and cyberattacks. Remember, hackers love a good challenge—don't make it easy for them!

7. Contractor's Equipment Insurance:

This protects your tools and equipment from damage or theft because losing your power tools is not a fun day at the office!

Reputable Insurance Companies for Government Contractors

Ready to secure your coverage? Here are some reputable insurance companies that cater to government contractors:

1. The Hartford: [www.thehartford.com](https://www.thehartford.com)

2. Liberty Mutual: [www.libertymutual.com](https://www.libertymutual.com)

3. Travelers: [www.travelers.com](https://www.travelers.com)

4. Nationwide: [www.nationwide.com](https://www.nationwide.com)

5. Chubb: [www.chubb.com](https://www.chubb.com)

6. Berkshire Hathaway: [www.bh.com](https://www.bh.com)

7. AIG: [www.aig.com](https://www.aig.com)

8. Markel: [www.markel.com](https://www.markel.com)

9. Zurich: [www.zurichna.com](https://www.zurichna.com)

10. CNA: [www.cna.com](https://www.cna.com)

Conclusion

Navigating the insurance landscape as a government contractor may feel like trying to read a novel in a foreign language, but it's essential for your success and survival in the contracting game. With the right coverage, you'll be well-equipped to tackle the challenges that come your way and ensure that your business can weather any storm. Remember, as the wise Benjamin Franklin once said, "An ounce of prevention is worth a pound of cure." So gear up, grab that insurance, and let's dive into the world of federal contracting like the savvy entrepreneur you are!

---

Case Study 1: The Construction Catastrophe

Background:

A small construction company, *BuildRight Co.*, secured a federal contract to renovate a local government building. Excited about the opportunity, the owner, Jake, decided to save money by opting out of general liability insurance, believing that his experienced crew would prevent any accidents.

The Incident:

During the renovation, one of Jake's workers accidentally damaged a neighboring property when a piece of equipment fell, causing significant damage to the fence and landscape. The homeowner filed a claim against *BuildRight Co.*, seeking compensation for repairs.

Consequences:

Without insurance to cover the damages, Jake found himself personally liable for the costs. The repairs amounted to over $50,000, which he had to pay out of pocket. This financial hit not only drained his savings but also put his business at risk. Unable to absorb such a loss, *BuildRight Co.* struggled to stay afloat and ultimately had to withdraw from the federal contracting space, losing future opportunities and credibility in the industry.

Key Takeaway:

Jake learned the hard way that saving a few dollars on insurance can lead to catastrophic financial consequences. As he put it, "I thought I could handle the risks, but one mistake put me out of business. Never again will I skip on insurance."

---

Case Study 2: The IT Mishap

Background:

*DataSecure Solutions*, a small IT firm, landed a lucrative government contract to provide cybersecurity solutions for a federal agency. The owner, Lisa, felt confident in her team's abilities and opted to forgo cyber liability insurance, assuming that her robust security measures would prevent any breaches.

The Incident:

A few months into the project, a sophisticated cyberattack targeted the agency's systems, exploiting a vulnerability in the software *DataSecure Solutions* had implemented. Sensitive data was compromised, leading to a significant breach that required extensive remediation.

Consequences:

The federal agency held *DataSecure Solutions* responsible for the breach, leading to a lawsuit that sought damages for the costs incurred due to the breach. Lisa faced not only hefty legal fees but also the potential loss of her contract with the government. The total costs exceeded $200,000, and without insurance, she had no safety net to fall back on. Ultimately, the incident tarnished her reputation, making it almost impossible to secure future contracts.

Key Takeaway:

Lisa's experience highlighted the critical importance of cyber liability insurance, especially in the IT sector. As she reflected, "I thought my security was enough, but when it came to liability, I realized I was playing with fire. The loss was more than just financial; it was my credibility in the industry."

---

**Conclusion**

Both case studies illustrate the significant risks and consequences that can arise from not having the appropriate insurance coverage as a government contractor. From financial ruin to loss of credibility, the absence of insurance can lead to disastrous outcomes that extend beyond mere monetary loss. The lessons learned by Jake and Lisa serve as cautionary tales for all contractors entering the federal contracting space. As the saying goes, "Better safe than sorry!"

# Disclaimer:

The information provided in this book is intended to serve as a general guide to federal contracting and its associated sectors. Please be aware that regulations and policies related to federal contracting can change frequently. As such, the content herein may not reflect the most current laws, regulations, or guidelines.

For the most up-to-date information regarding federal contracting regulations, requirements, and procedures, we strongly recommend that readers consult the relevant government agency or department directly. This will ensure that you have access to the latest data and compliance requirements necessary for successful participation in federal contracting. Always verify information with official sources to stay informed and compliant.

Made in the USA
Columbia, SC
30 October 2024

45355073R00072